MW00477996

45

ALSO BY SCOTT DIKKERS AND
PETER HILLEREN

*Destined for Destiny: The Unauthorized
Autobiography of George W. Bush*

45

A Portrait of
My Knucklehead Brother Jeb

George W. Bush

Actually written by
Scott Dikkers
and Peter Hilleren

GRAND CENTRAL
PUBLISHING

NEW YORK   BOSTON

This book is a parody and has not been prepared, approved, endorsed, or authorized by George W. Bush

Copyright © 2015 by Scott Dikkers and Peter Hilleren
All rights reserved. In accordance with the U.S. Copyright Act of 1976, the scanning, uploading, and electronic sharing of any part of this book without the permission of the publisher constitute unlawful piracy and theft of the author's intellectual property. If you would like to use material from the book (other than for review purposes), prior written permission must be obtained by contacting the publisher at permissions@hbgusa.com. Thank you for your support of the author's rights.

Grand Central Publishing
Hachette Book Group
1290 Avenue of the Americas
New York, NY 10104

www.HachetteBookGroup.com

Printed in the United States of America

RRD-C

First Edition: November 2015
10 9 8 7 6 5 4 3 2 1

Grand Central Publishing is a division of Hachette Book Group, Inc.
The Grand Central Publishing name and logo is a trademark of Hachette Book Group, Inc.

The Hachette Speakers Bureau provides a wide range of authors for speaking events. To find out more, go to www.hachettespeakersbureau.com or call (866) 376-6591.

The publisher is not responsible for websites (or their content) that are not owned by the publisher.

Library of Congress Cataloging-in-Publication Data

Dikkers, Scott.
   45 : a portrait of my knucklehead brother Jeb : a parody / by George W. Bush with Scott Dikkers and Peter Hilleren.—First edition
      pages cm
   ISBN 978-1-4555-9285-2 (hardback)—ISBN 978-1-4789-6235-9 (audio download)—ISBN 978-1-4789-6236-6 (audio cd) 1. Bush, Jeb—Humor. 2. Governors—Florida—Humor. 3. Florida—Politics and government—1951—Humor. 4. Presidential candidates—United States—Humor. 5. Bush, George W. (George Walker), 1946—Parodies, imitations, etc. I. Hilleren, Peter. II. Bush, George W. (George Walker), 1946- 41. III. Title. IV. Title: Forty-five.
   F316.23.B87D55 2015
   975.9'063092—dc23
                                    2015028832

To myself

Contents

45

How Can One Man Write More Than One Book?

———⌀∿⌀———

My name is George W. Bush. You may know me from my beautiful paintings, which were on display in the fall of 2012 at the prestigious Dallas–Fort Worth Museum of Art & *Walker, Texas Ranger* Memorabilia. I believe the works shown in that exhibit received a citation of some kind, and I'm quite certain the show was written up in the local newspapers.

You may also be familiar with me through my other literature writings: the book I wrote about my relationship with my father, *41: A Portrait of My Father*; my superb unauthorized autobiography, *Destined for Destiny*; and the inspiring account of my great leadership of a nation, *Decision Points*.

Oh, and that reminds me. You may also remember me serving as the forty-third President of the United States. I was on the TV during that time.

The book you are holding now, which was legitimately written by me, is, oddly, not about me. At least, not directly. Rest assured I am featured prominently in the pages ahead. But mostly, this is a book about my brother Jeb, who is slated to be the forty-fifth President of the United States.

Now, at this point, you are probably asking yourself, "When do I get to see some of these renowned paintings you mentioned ever so coyly at the beginning of the chapter?" and I cannot blame you. Usually books of this type, profiles of a candidate released in the heat of a presidential campaign, are simply a candidate's "handlers'" attempt to cast the office-runner in a positive light, which means these books are often, shall we say, light on the substanceness. They are also a publisher's attempt to exploit the notoriety of a candidate. In short, such books are self-serving tripe written in a few days to not only help a candidate, but make a quick dollar.

In my defense, I must point out that this is not a self-serving book. It is a "Jeb-serving" book. It was, however, written in a few days, and I sincerely hope it makes a great deal of quick dollars.

But, why else am I writing this book?

Shortly after Jeb's last birthday, my father, the forty-first President of these United States, George H. W. Bush, wrote me a heartfelt letter, imploring me to tout the virtues of my younger brother. And I'm not going to lie. It brought a tear to my eye. And it left me no room to waver. When my father gives me a directive, I follow it. Below are the letters of the letter he sent me. See if it doesn't pull at your heartstrings as it did mine.

Originally I thought of helping Jeb become President by creating a type of coffee-table book filled with reproductions of my beautiful full-color paintings. Through these paintings I would show my brother's fitness for the chief office of our country. The paintings would, through color, texture, and brushstroke, inspire the mind of the beholder to understand everything a prospective American voter would need to know about a Jeb Bush administration, its detailed policy proposals, and why I support them.

I have been painting for quite some time now, and in fact I now

FROM THE DESK OF
GEORGE. H. W. BUSH

George,

Help Jeb get elected. Maybe write a book?

George H. W. Bush

George H. W. Bush

prefer to communicate through art instead of through writing or words, when possible. For example, when dining out, I will point to a picture of the food I want on the menu. If there are no pictures, I will quickly paint a picture of the entree and give it to my waiter. Usually, it is a painting of hot dogs and Tater Tots, which takes a great deal of skill and patience to paint.

Customer service calls to my local cable company are particularly challenging for me, since they take place over the phone. First, I paint a painting that captures the particular issue I need help with, be it an issue with my bill, or something having to do with technical support, such as the cable box not working properly. Then I call them and proceed to describe the painting to the customer service associate in great detail. So far this has not been a successful communication strategy, as the person on the phone usually asks repeatedly and insistently for me to explain my concern in words as opposed to interpreting my own visual art, and the person quickly hangs up on me when they realize I will only be describing my painting. But I will not alter my course. I will continue with this strategy until I can watch the DIY channel, which is currently a black screen. Are you reading this, cable helper people?

But my father, who thinks art is hogwash, urged me to reconsider the painting idea and write a book of words instead. Here is the impassioned note I received to that effect:

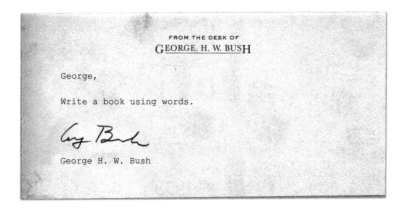

After receiving that touching message, I had a new course. I resolved to undertake the hard work of writing this book.

Regardlessly, I could not help myself, and created the paintings anyway. They are reproduced in these pages, somewhere around the middle of the book. Those with more of a mind to the arts than to the written word may prefer to simply look at the paintings. For those who cannot read, the paintings will do the job nicely. If you are blind, you are encouraged to purchase the audiobook edition of *45*, which will contain a helpful section in which I describe the paintings in great detail. My in-depth analysis of the artwork will, in fact, comprise roughly 90 percent of the audiobook.

All that aside, if you are not blind, do not like looking at paintings, or simply prefer words, please continue reading.

In this book, I will lay out my thoughts about Jeb's suitability for the job of commander in chief. I have known him his whole life and have seen him tested in ways the nation never will. Being an older brother, I have viciously tortured Jeb for most of his life. And he deserved it, because he is a bonehead. The question we must ask for the future of our nation, however, is, "How will such a fat dope earn the highest command chair in the land?" It will be a torturous journey for him, filled with Indian burns, nipple twists, and noogies. But through this trial, we will see whether he emerges destined to become "45."

Enjoy these readings.

The Birth of Jeb, a Legend in Birthery

————ᴄᴠɔ————

I'll be honest with you. Before Jeb came along, I had no need of a brother. Life was pretty good all by myself. I enjoyed the unfettered attentions of my father, through his loving writing of very concise notes, and of my mother, through her polite howls of "Just give me a moment of peace, please!" I played among the dirt patches and dried grasses of Midland, Texas, happy as can be.

In this hot, dry paradise I felt like I had the run of the place. I hurled baseballs through windows, tortured my fair share of frogs, and stained or otherwise damaged many freshly installed carpets. Why should I want a brother to share in any of this childhood magic? I surely didn't.

Frankly, I still don't.

Nevertheless, very soon my mother's belly was about to burst with a new baby brother for me, and I did not want it. So, being the mischievous boy I was, I set my mind to figuring out a way to get rid of this baby.

I thought if I could just poke the baby, that would likely dispatch it, like when you poke a mouse really hard. Sadly, I wasn't allowed near any sharp or flammable objects. There had been an incident with the dog involving kabob sticks, and another incident involving fireworks and the lawn mower. There were surely other incidents as well. The main point being I was not allowed near anything flammable, sharp, breakable, fragile, long, new, or white.

But before I could figure out a method of getting rid of this future brother, I had more basic problems to solve. For example, where was the baby, exactly? I had learned that a stork would bring the new baby to the family, yet as my mother's belly began to grow, and she and others spoke of the baby as somehow being in her belly, this confused me greatly. Was the baby in the sky, being carried by a terrifying, shrieking beast, or was it inside my mother? Or both?

At the tender age of seven, I did not yet know about the complexities of stork-human reproduction, or the intricate way in which mighty fowl delivered babies to mothers' stomachs already in swaddling blankets, using both their powerful beaks and perhaps piercing talons as well, to place the baby inside the stomach, or, as I later learned to call it, the womb.

I asked some of my friends in school, and they contrived impossible horrors that could only serve to poison the mind of a young boy. One boy led me to believe that a stork had disgraced my mother, and I cried and cried, then ran home and demanded that my mother tell me it wasn't true. She simply asked me to quiet down, as I recall. But I was resolute. I was angry at the stork, and vowed to hunt down and destroy the bird. I am still searching for it. It has been a lifelong hunt.

But that is a subject for another book.

My mother tried to explain the entire situation to me, but grew weary of her inability to articulate it in a way a seven-year-old could understand. My father's handwritten notes avoided the topic altogether.

It would be a long time before I understood the processes and procedures of bringing children into this world. Even today, the finer points confound me. Laura seems to know, but will not divulge her womanly secrets. When it was time for her to bring the girls into our lives, she went to a wonderful place in the hospital where only ladies are allowed, and that's where she was handed the babies, presumably by a higher-station stork with medical credentials. I was handed them later, but did not meet the bird.

So, this is as much as I have been able to glean. God fits into it somewhere, to implant the soul, but I still do not understand when that happens precisely. I can only speculate that the storks and the Lord have a strategic partnership that is special in both the animal kingdom and the Bible. Bees are also somehow involved. And the growing of cabbages is also an integral component of the science, as I understand it.

There are many mysteries that our finest minds and our greatest doctors have not fully uncovered in this world. The miracle of child-birth is one of them. And I prefer to leave mysteries to the philoso-phizers. A curious mind only leads to trouble.

All that presiding, the immediate problem of seven-year-old George W. Bush remained: How was I going to get rid of this baby?

My effort to somehow prevent the birth of my brother was dealt another blow when, after my mother became visibly pregnant, she adopted a new twelve-foot rule. I was not allowed within twelve feet of her at all times. She was not feeling well, and apparently the energy it took to continually bellow, "Be quiet," "That's enough," and "George, stop it!" took too great a toll on her constitution, and she could not withstand being disturbed in any way. I understood the new rule. I knew she loved me because the nanny told me, but I began to envy my new unborn brother because he got to spend all of his time with her. The twelve-foot rule was unfair, and unjust.

One night during this time, I had a powerful dream. I felt a gentle touch on my hand. I opened my eyes to find a beautiful mermaid floating before me. I surmised this dream had taken me to the underwater kingdom of Atlantis!

A voice bellowed, "I am Poseidon! Who has trespassed in my kingdom?"

I then noticed the mermaid had a rich, full beard. Poseidon's long, waving hair was most likely what confused me into thinking he was a mermaid. He was, nonetheless, still strangely beautiful.

"I'm George W. Bush, sir," I said.

Poseidon seemed taken aback. "George W. Bush, the second-greatest US President ever?"

Being seven, I surmised that this was complete nonsense.

"Where are my toys? Are we having hot dogs and macaroni and cheese for dinner? I want to go home now."

"You're going to have a younger brother," Poseidon spokefied. "You're going to have to guide him and lead him. He might one day be the greatest President of the United States."

"Ever!" he added.

The merman was trying to put a lot of weight on my young shoulders, and I didn't feel up to it.

"I can't even tie my shoes by myself!" I cried.

"Whether he achieves this high office will be up to you, and you alone."

"I want to wake up now! Where's my BB gun?"

Poseidon sighed, "Yes, wake up if you want. It's your dream. Your lucky numbers are forty-one, forty-three, forty-five, nine, and eleven."

I awoke, and to my great dismay I was no longer in the dazzling, emerald-encrusted undersea kingdom. I was in my plain old bedroom.

When I regained my senses, I knew my life was to be different from this point forward. I had a new purpose. I had a new calling. My seven-year-old mind did not understand it, but my modern-day mind does. So, retroactively, I realized my life's purpose in the past that day, and set out from the future on what I knew then I would know now to be my new old young life's purpose: to help my baby brother Jeb on his journey, to forge a leader who would be worthy of the President's chair.

And that is the central concern that must be determined: Will Jeb be worthy? Will I properly guide him on his journey? This is what this book will attempt to discover.

My new baby brother might one day be a great leader—and it would be up to me. Would I teach the baby Jeb what it needed to know to become a great leader? Or would I merely dismiss the infant as an annoyance? Would my one-day book ferret out the answers needed for Jeb to succeed? Would the book make the bestseller list? Would Jeb ever read the book?

There are too many questions to answer. So, we should not try to answer them.

As the day of Jeb's birth approached, my mother became more and more distant. The nanny explained to me that there would soon be a new baby in the house, and I would need to be very responsible with this new life. That would be easy now with my new mission. Instead of trying to get rid of this baby, I would now nurture it and tutor it. I began a concerted effort to demonstrate my ability to care for the child.

I gathered all of my favorite books, like *The ABC's* and *Bible Stories Heavily Edited for Children*, so that I could read them to the baby. I built a rudimentary podium out of Lincoln Logs, so that the baby could learn to be a powerful and persuasive public talker.

From that point on, I also began to address the baby in the womb.

I had to yell because of the twelve-foot rule, but yell I did. I yelled all about the exciting adventures we would have as brothers outside the womb. I promise-yelled that I would watch out for him, and teach him all about being a Bush. I sang-yelled lullabies at night until my mother's pained pleas of "George, shut up, for the love of Jesus!" could almost drown me out. I yelled so much praise and adoration at this new-life baby-thing that I actually began to believe all of it myself. I would lose my voice frequently at that time because of all the yelling. And I would use the downtime to plan new yells.

One day when I came home from school, my mother wasn't in her usual "ladies' comfort" reclining chair. I searched the house, but the nanny told me that my newborn sibling was coming, and when my mother returned she would do so with baby Jeb in her arms.

I paced the house, wondering if my yell-bonding would bear fruit. I could not sleep, and I could not eat.

Eventually, late into the next day, my father's limousine arrived to take me to visit my mom and new brother, Jeb. He then told me through a very touching handwritten note that Jeb hadn't slept since he was born late the previous night. Jeb had been crying and crying, and doctors were worried that something was wrong with him. I began to have a good feeling.

When Dad brought me to the isolated room where they were keeping Jeb, I heard the wailing down the hall. We stepped into the room, where a nurse was futilely cradling the infant, cooing like a dove in an effort to soothe him. I knew what I had to do. I yelled as loud as I could: "*Quiet, Jeb! I'm here!*" Instantly, the baby went silent, his tiny arms flailing excitedly. "*Go to sleep, Jeb!*" I yelled, and Jeb instantly closed his eyes and began tiny-snoring.

My strategy had worked. The baby was confused and frightened in this strange new world without my voice to guide him.

My astonished father wrote me a note that night that simply said, "It seems you have the magic touch, Georgie. We're going to put you two in the same room."

My plan had succeeded. Now a lifetime of presidential training could begin.

A Younger Brother in Need of Careful Taunting

———— ✺ ————

By any measure the upbringing Jeb shared with me was a very normal American childhood. Like anybody, we often hosted secret Skull and Bones gatherings at our home with my father's friends from college. Like in other homes, my dad would wear his robe and chant cryptic Satanic spells while opening the ancient tomb in our secret second basement. As my dad began climbing the political ladder, the household became busy with more intricate Freemason rituals, bloodlettings, and animal sacrifices—all the ordinary fixtures of everyday American life in those days. On weekends we'd have masked Illuminati sex parties where international financiers, royalty, and eccentric felons would indulge in wanton hedonistic dalliances by candlelight. Tuesday was Parcheesi night, and there was often a nice door prize for the winner.

But Jeb and I were oblivious to most of this boring grown-up business, of course. Like most kids, we went about our own affairs in our own sphere. And in that spherically shaped circle, Jeb was a leader in training, and I was the trainer training the trainee. With superb trainings.

I would wake Jeb every morning well before dawn by screaming at him, *"Wake up, Jeb!"* I began this when Jeb was still an infant in his crib, and continued the practice throughout his childhood. In fact, I do it to this day, but with technology such as it is, I now phone Jeb every morning around four thirty and scream at him to wake up. It works well, and it always helps him get a good jump on his day.

But in the times of our youth, our days were spent together.

One of my favorite pastimes as a boy was torturing frogs. When Jeb came along, I realized I had a much more interesting victim. It was fun for me, providing great amusement as I tormented this funny fat infant, but I also knew, or at least know now, and knew then that I would know now, at least in terms of knowing what I knew at that time as compared to my future knowledge unknowable in the before-time, that by mistreating him greatly, I would steel him against the enemies of this world. My cruel behavior would make him strong. It was tough love. Torture-love, you could call it.

One of my favorite ways to do this was to taunt baby Jeb while he was enjoying milk from his bottle. I would watch him carefully as he slurped the milk, sucking his little wet lips in and out. Then, at just the right moment, I would pop the bottle out of his mouth. His little face would tighten up and turn red, and his little lip would quiver, and he would let out a big cry for his milk. It was good fun, and I enjoyed hours of laughter from this simple game.

Another helpful thing I would do, when no one was looking, is that I would swat Jeb in the face, hard. He would cry and cry. His face was puffy and swollen so often from my punches and slaps that it became that way permanently, hence the wide doughy face that folks know and love today. Jeb also lost all sensitivity in his jaw and cheeks, which has served him well throughout the years. Dentists are often astounded at his near-superhuman ability to withstand the searing pain of invasive dental procedures without the need of Novocain.

Some of the important training activities I oversaw would garner the attention of my mother, who would sometimes come to investigate when Jeb was screaming and crying. I would always deny that I had done anything.

"He just started crying," I would say. "I didn't do anything." This seemed to me at the time to be an absolutely solid alibi. And in fact, even to this day, the statement strikes me as a superb defense. I do not understand how anyone could doubt it. It is a clear statement denying wrongdoing, and it is airtight. But somehow, my mother figured out that I had hit Jeb or taken his milk, and she would give me a sound walloping.

She did not understand the important work I was doing.

As he grew, I continued to sucker punch Jeb. He often had a bruised shoulder or a bloody nose. I knew that eventually, these various pummelings would instill in Jeb a deep understanding of the importance of a strong national defense.

I helped Jeb learn to walk. I felt it was my duty to teach him this much-needed skill. Those who cannot walk cannot lead. Some may disagree, pointing to the great FDR, who served four terms as President in a wheelchair. But this is a misnomer of history. As soon as he lost the use of his legs due to Polio, FDR resigned from the Presidency, leaving our nation in the capable hands of his Vice President, John Nance Garner. FDR then vanished from public life, selling apples on the street from his wheelchair during the Great Depression, assuming the transgendered identity "Betty."

By the time he was one years old, Jeb had learned to crawl. But in my mind, crawling was beneath a future leader befitting the portent of my dream. So I took Jeb out to the front yard, which was filled with prickly nettle plants and Mexican Prickly Poppy growing close to the ground. Jeb was wearing a diaper and shoes and nothing else. I set him down and walked away. Of course being trained as he was, he tried to follow me. He would get a couple of feet, and inevitably his hand or knee would hit a nettle—you should have heard the howling! He would try crawling again and the same thing would happen.

Well, as you can imagine, this broke him of the crawling habit real quick. Well, kind of quick. It was after a few days of this when he finally tried to stand. But he quickly fell to his hands and knees given that he had not developed any sense of balance. Eventually, after about a month in those sharp weeds, he got the idea, and was lurching along on two feet. It was a proud day for us both.

This trial of learning to walk taught Jeb the importance of wearing shoes, which every respected leader must do. In all my years as President, I never appeared barefoot. Nor did I encounter any other head of state who went barefoot. It simply isn't done. And this is a vital fact for Jeb to know.

Through the years, I instinctively knew to teach Jeb survival skills—things he would need to know in the real world, like how to survive being randomly tortured. Every day I would come up with different surprise-hurts. It started out with wet willies and pantsings. It advanced to a bit of showerboarding, playing music in his room extremely loudly and at late hours so he could not sleep for days on end, cracker crumbs in his bed, and other horrors.

As I grew into a teenager and my own activities such as baseball and dating kept me busier and busier, I made up a schedule to keep up with Jeb's pain training. Our daily schedule had at least three "enhanced-taunting" techniques planned, one physical (such as Indian burns or wedgies), one psychological (such as repeating everything he said for several weeks, or telling him our parents had moved away), and one random (such as a spider in his oatmeal). Jeb grew into a resilient young man. He got so he couldn't even feel the glass shards I put in his shoes! And he still has a healthy fear of toilets after the many swirlies he endured. This is a foundational quality in a leader.

Some of my most cherished childhood memories are of tormenting Jeb, thereby molding him into the man he is today. For example, when we went out bigfoot hunting in the woods when Jeb was no more than three years old, I ditched him, leaving him to muster the fortitude to find his own way back home by himself. I did this repeatedly, and Jeb fell for it every time. He was gone for several days one time. Since he so often hid in his bedroom for days at a stretch to avoid my rigorous trainings, neither our family nor the maidservants thought anything of his absence. When he finally found his way home, stumbling in, covered in dirt, scratches, and mosquito bites— as well as a tick that had reached the size of a walnut attached to his thigh—I told Mom and Dad that he had fallen. And they were never the wiser.

These adventures in the woods taught Jeb the importance of properly managing our nation's natural resources, and caring for our environment.

Over time, more of my leadership lessons began to take hold. When we shared a bedroom, I noted how Jeb had demonstrated superb leadership over his half of the room. We often had conflicts over disputed regions, such as the dresser drawers, closet shelf space, and the toilet bowl. But Jeb engaged in negotiations with the proper respect when I laid him down, kneeled on his back, and twisted his arm the wrong way. He always accepted my decree that such contested spaces were official protectorates of my half of the room.

When he was eight years old, Jeb got his first pet, a pet fish, which he named Herman. He adored that fish. Like a wise leader tending to his people, he took care of his little pet fish with great care, tenderness, and attention to detail, until I made him eat it.

And Jeb was an excellent student in school, learning all of the math, science, reading, and writing that would be of no use to him as a world leader.

It wasn't all business with me and Jeb, though. We played lots of games as well: dodgeball, dustball, and tarball. When there was no tar available for the ball, Jeb would stand in. My friends and I would coat his whole body with hot oil and kick and shove him through our opponents' goal. It wasn't easy—Jeb was quite chubby! But it was the joy of kicking Jeb that made the game so much fun.

As Jeb got older, I felt it was time to teach him an appreciation of how our economy works, so I took him under my business wing. We would collect money from investors (usually Dad) to build a lemonade stand or the like. We'd then buy a piece of signboard, write "Lemonade: 5¢" on it, then we'd get a folding table from the garage, tape the sign to it, and put it by the road. After a week or so of ignoring the table, we'd declare bankruptcy and spend all of Dad's investment money on other things. Then we would ask him to bail out our failed business. We did the same with "Car Wash: $5" and "Hot Doggies: $2" with increasingly large investments from our father. It believe it gave my dad a strong sense of pride when I'd inform him of my latest bankruptcy, which was often followed by an enormous bailout.

"George and Jeb are natural businessmen!" he would exclaim gleefully.

By the time Jeb went out on his own to college, he was ready. He had developed quick reflexes and a sixth sense for danger, dodging and swinging at anyone who came up behind him. He would do a ten-point check of his dormitory room before going to bed every night, scouting for intruders, invisible gases, and sharp objects in his chairs and bed. He checked the underside of his car for cut brake lines, potatoes in the exhaust pipe, and homemade explosives. He would offer food to others to taste first in case of poisoning.

That first day Jeb managed to avoid all of my scheduled tribulations was a milestone. I gave him a torture diploma and an "I survived George" T-shirt, and sent him on his way. I was confident that he was ready to face the real world.

Columba: Un Amor Que Se Hace Arriba Por Completo

———— ⌀ ————

For most boys, the teen years are a time for having a few dates, working up the nerve to hold hands and maybe smooch a girl, and generally building the kind of confidence you might need if you ever met the right girl and wanted to court her like a gentleman and make her a bride.

Not Jeb.

Jeb was hopeless with women. He was a paste-eater, and a hard-luck case besides. When it came to matters of the heart, Jeb stuttered and fumbled and generally made a mess of things from beginning to end.

A natural-born bumbler, Jeb would often botch even the simplest gesture of affection toward a girl at school.

There was a girl named Florence Whitzaker, for example, in the fifth grade. Jeb was in her class, and he took a liking to her. But he had the dumbest idea for how to show her. He waited for her to use the drinking fountain at school so he could take advantage of the opportunity to be chivalrous and cradle her head to help her drink the water. But since Jeb is a lummox who doesn't know his own strength, he gripped her head in his powerful rail-splitter-sized hands and proceeded to bang her head against the spout and hold it there, knocking out her front teeth and almost drowning the poor girl. She cried and cried and ran all the way home. Jeb was mortified, barely understanding what had happened.

Another time, in the ninth grade, Jeb decided that he would ask Eugenia Derndtshaw to go to the prom with him. Leave it to ol' sawdust-for-brains Jeb to turn this simple act into a complicated ordeal. He had an elaborate plan to ask her in view of her whole family, to make it more difficult for her to refuse. He followed her home from school and hid in the bushes outside the family's dining room, waiting for her large family to be seated for dinner together. He then tried to climb through the dining room window, but he was too big to fit, and got stuck. As he tried to wriggle free, he broke the window. The Derndtshaws' dog went crazy, and ran outside and tore at Jeb's dangling feet, and even tore a chunk out of the rear end of his trousers. The Midland police were called. The family—the entire community—was embarrassed, repulsed, and a little bit frightened by the incident.

To add insult to injury, the Derndtshaw girl said no. To a Bush! I know that Jeb is no great prize, but mishap or no, she should have been honored to be asked, and done the right thing by accepting. In light of this disturbing turn of events, our father sent her a very nice note:

FROM THE DESK OF
GEORGE. H. W. BUSH

Dear Eugenia,

Please accept Jeb's request and accompany him to the prom.

Warmest personal regards,

George H. W. Bush, U.S. Congressman, 7th District

And she still refused! I believe he later asked CIA operatives to dispatch her in a mysterious car accident, but that is another story.

The long and short of it is that this is the kind of luck Jeb typically had with women. Not only was he unlucky in love—he was a certified disaster-case.

So toward the end of his high-school years, when Jeb started telling stories of a romance he was having with a mysterious sixteen-year-old girl south of the border whom no one had ever seen, everyone—me, my friends, even Jeb's friends—naturally assumed that this was a made-up girlfriend.

"Oh sure, Jeb—you have a mysterious Mexican girlfriend who is a hot Latin dance machine!" we joked.

We laughed it off and let Jeb have his fantasy, for the most part. We ribbed him a little, of course—snickering at him behind his back when he earnestly told of his feelings for the sultry foreign lover of his imaginings—but mostly, we didn't bother. There were much bigger, dumber things Jeb did that deserved more-dedicated ridicule. He was such a funny dumb dope that no matter what he did, it was good for a laugh. Every day was a gift from Jeb of a new dumb thing he said or did.

After a while, talk of this pretend Mexican girlfriend got more detailed, and the conceit grew more intricate. She had a name now, "Columba"—clearly a name invented by Jeb, I thought. He would leave for days at a stretch to presumably spend time with her, getting to know her family, and courting her.

I assumed he was, in actuality, driving down to the seed mill and hanging around by himself in those empty, darkened pole sheds for days on end, just killing time to make it seem like he had truly gone to Mexico. Meanwhile, he was hoping this would convince everyone that the made-up stories of his great new love were true. That was just the kind of dunderheaded type of thing Jeb would always do. So, I thought nothing of it.

Imagine my surprise one warm spring day when Jeb showed up at our house with a ravishing caramel-skinned creature on his arm, appearing to be the Mexican lover of his dreams.

I could not believe it.

Jeb droned on in his big dumb voice about how he had met this "love of his life" and how it had been like a bolt of lightning—love at first sight, or some nonsense.

I had great difficulty suppressing my snickering, because I knew what had really happened: Jeb was going all the way with this charade. He had already made up so many lies, even gone on his bogus "trips" to Mexico, and here he was upping the ante: He had gone so far as to find someone to play the part of his mystery girlfriend. Who this girl was and why she would agree to do this, I did not know, but one thing is for certain: Jeb really knows how to double down on a fib.

He started "dating" this woman more regularly. At least, that's what he said. I knew he was still just hanging out in those pole sheds, twiddling his thumbs. Then he would come back from several days of crushing boredom and solitude and tell us how he had so much fun "going out on a date" with Columba, meeting her family, and having a wild time in Mexico.

How convenient it was that this woman could not speak a word of English! We sure would have liked to ask her a few questions, like, "How much is Jeb paying you to act as his girlfriend?" or, "Are you being held against your will?" My folks, especially, were concerned for the poor girl's safety, knowing as they did Jeb's proclivity for unintended brutishness, like the time he crushed the cat by hugging it too hard.

But Jeb never blinked. He kept up this act, year after year. He even staged an illegitimate marriage with the girl. Maybe she thought she was acting in a movie scene or something. That is a theory one of Jeb's buddies had—that Jeb had told her he was a movie director who would make her a star, and whenever he brought her up to Texas, they were shooting scenes for his great epic. I thought this was a pretty good theory, and I chose to accept it as fact for a time.

Our whole family attended the wedding, and was greatly confused, my parents particularly. In the final synthesis, they only wanted Jeb to be happy, and if he was happy continuing this myth that he had an exotic love from a faraway land that no one could speak to, that made no nevermind to them.

As he settled into his sham marriage, Jeb seemed happy. Again, I was not there at his house at every moment, so I can only assume he lived alone and spent most of his time sitting in his underpants, watching daytime TV and eating reheated macaroni and cheese and tuna all day, just like he had done growing up. He presumably only called for this actress—who even knows what her real name is— when there was a family gathering or holiday meal to attend.

Things got complicated when Jeb began bringing children to meet the family. The children appeared to be half-white, half-Mexican, so he truly went all out to make sure they matched children that he and this woman might have had, were they a legitimate married couple. My mind was greatly perplexed. Many of us wondered where the children had come from. Surely conscripting them into his elaborate ruse would be much more difficult than finding a willing adult. It's possible they were orphans that Jeb adopted, and then he hired a nanny to look after them while he was eating macaroni and cheese and tuna and watching TV by himself.

Once the children grew, we can only assume that Jeb could have found young Mexican-American actors who could convincingly play his children. I believe any competent young person from Mexico gifted in the performing arts could pull that off. All they would have to do is stand around and recite some simple lines in English like, "My name is José Bush," or what have you.

These children are grown now, and many of them have achieved some success politically. One of them was recently elected to a state-wide office in Florida.

In the meanwhiles, I am wondering if and when the other shoe will drop. When are these children, or this "wife"—who are likely to become America's first fake First Family—going to come out and admit that they are a front for my brother's inability to score with women?

Jeb continues to confide in me the original conceit of this whole web of lies—he will periodically lean into me and whisper, "She is a real tiger." As a brother and as a man, I understand what he is trying to say, but of course I know in my heart it is only a part of his big sad lie. I know that Jeb has never had carnal relations with this woman. He in fact has never had carnal relations with any woman. He remains innocent in the ways of the flesh. He is too big of a stumble-bum to ever know such earthly pleasures. And this poor woman who plays the role of his bride likely has a nice, loving husband and fine children of her own somewhere, whom she enjoys visiting when she is not doing the sad job of standing around Jeb, collecting an off-the-books paycheck.

If Jeb's marriage charade proves one thing, it is this: He can pull off a serious, high-profile cover-up, a quality that will serve him well should he become the President of a United State.

What Are Jeb's Business Failures? And Why They Don't Matter!

———— ०ᐧᴐ ————

Before he became a Governor, Jeb had a very successful career in a job that not a lot of folks know about. This career I am speaking of, Jeb's chosen line of work, is that of getting lots of money from other people without doing anything, losing that money, and then making a great deal of profit in the process. In his illustrious getting-money-from-other-people career, Jeb has climbed his way up the company ladder, at first working closely with gullible small investors, then bloated private corporations who didn't notice how he would siphon their money away and, finally, our father's office at the White House, which always proved a willing partner. Jeb has had a very lucrative-ful career.

In most families, this would be a source of great pride. But in the Bush family, it is a source of grave concern.

You see, failing at business—and failing big—is a long-standing Bush tradition.

Look at my brother Neil, for example. He failed splendidly with a Denver-area savings and loan in the 1980s that led to a federal investigation, lawsuits, and ultimately criminal charges. When the bottom fell out of the entire savings and loan industry, Neil's business was the recipient of a bailout of over a billion dollars, thanks to the hardworking American taxpayer.

Everyone in the Bush family is very proud of Neil.

For another good example, take a look at me. Prior to my career in politics, I was involved in two charmingly doomed oil-industry businesses: Arbusto Energy and Spectrum 7. Both companies lost a lot of money and went bankrupt very quickly.

Everyone in the Bush family is very proud of me as well.

Key to any understanding of these impressive failures is that, in the case of both Neil and myself, as our business ventures crumbled around us, leaving our investors high and dry and our workers out on the street, we personally made a great deal of money. As accusations of negligence, impropriety, and incompetence flew at us from every direction, we sat back comfortably from these enriching collapses, smiling at the sweet smell of failure. Neil walked away with a hefty salary increase, bonuses, and off-the-books loans. I managed to get extremely lucky and sell the stock in my companies just moments before they went belly-up.

Profiting from such beautiful, colossal failures is, in many ways, the Bush family business. Every business must make a profit in order to make shareholders happy. But in a Bush family business, great profits come from great failures.

And that is where Jeb falls short.

His businesses are certainly all sketchy, somewhat fly-by-night in nature. After he leaves a company, a trail of lawsuits, fines, and accusations of criminal wrongdoing often follow. He has always followed up his superb failures with heroic bailouts and last-minute golden-parachute escapes that bear the distinct mark of his name. All of these things are commendable, and in line with family tradition. However, there is one way in which Jeb is not living up to that tradition: Many of his businesses have not crashed and burned spectacularly. Many of them still exist. Some of them continue to attract big-money investors. And that is troubling.

Jeb still has a lot to learn. He has time to make things right, and learn to properly fail at business. And I believe he can.

When I worked with him on the lemonade stands of our youth, he learned that the way a business works is that you get a large investment, spend all of the money, slip out the back door while the company is imploding, and then reap a large profit in the form of bailout money. It may seem like a small detail to a layperson that Jeb has not done particularly well at the "while it's imploding" part, but it is in many ways the most important part of the process of running a business. A businessman cannot succeed if his business does not fail.

I believe one of the reasons Jeb has not failed enough, or at least not quickly enough, is that he has always taken safe positions like "advisor" and "board trustee." Each of these positions would earn him lots of money for very little work. He would only be required to attend meetings a few times a year, and go on the occasional golfing trip and such. The problem was, these cushy positions weren't as boldly exposed as they needed to be to be remembered as grand, proud Bush failures. Jeb himself was personally removed from the giant red "fail" lever that they have next to the CEO's desk in the headquarters at every great company. Jeb left that to the partners and other executives he worked with. That was a big mistake. Jeb could never act, and pull that lever. In his business achievings, Jeb always seemed content on being nothing more than an "unseen player" and a "backroom dealer."

Jeb has, however, also served on the board of many companies that were sued for fraud, environmental violations, and a host of other crimes. He even allowed himself to be the middleman in a highly questionable real-estate firm that would later crumble in bankruptcy, the CEO heading to prison for twelve years. Another real-estate venture would see him working to help a partner defraud Medicare, a partner who is now a fugitive from justice. These are all good starts. But he would never let himself pull the trigger on letting it all come tumbling down. This may have been enough business acumen to get elected Governor of a backwater state like Florida, but a President has to set himself to a lower standard.

Therefore, recently, I took it upon myself to turn Jeb's business career around.

On the sly, I hooked Jeb up with a company that sold water pumps to struggling third-world nations. This is a bigger business than one might think, and the company I chose was egregiously misman- aged and corrupt, based in a country (Nigeria) that was even more egregiously mismanaged and corrupt than the business itself. All the right elements were in place. I encouraged Jeb to fly out to "negoti- ate" with officials, in at least one case with several suitcases full of cash. But somehow a "whistleblower," of which I deny being or even knowing about, alerted this shady deal to the Justice Department. Jeb made over a half a million on the deal. Not bad. Unfortunately, the company remains in business. I realized I had to go even further.

After he was through with his governorshipping, I used some influence with mutual friends to convince Jeb to start an investment business, which would have an excellent chance of failing once enor- mous amounts of money were invested, then squandered. Jeb got excited by the idea and created many investment companies. I was pleased that this may finally kick-start his flounderings. However, in the end he had a pretty disappointing failure rate, by Bush standards.

That just goes to show you the old saying, "You can't fail 'em all."

Many voters are impressed with Jeb's business acumen, and his business record. They compare it to mine. Has Jeb failed more than me? It's hard to say. We've each failed many times: me in Texas, Jeb in Florida, both of us worldwide. Though Jeb may have more failures than me, overall I believe my monetary losses are more impressive. And Jeb's failure trajectory has definitely flattened out since he left the Governor's office. So, I contend that Jeb still has more work to do to live up to my record.

But that is not the point of this book, or of any book that I am aware of. Jeb is his own failure, apart from all us other Bushes. Whether it was just dumb luck or spectacular business-failing genius, Jeb did it all on his own, despite my behind-the-scenes attempts to derail him to the finish line. Jeb's instincts for hooking up with shady characters and making extremely bad deals are uncanny. And he has learned the most important lesson: The key to a great business flop is to give it all you've got, and enjoy the process. This will serve him well if he is to become our President. Running the country is pretty much like running any business except there are missiles. It's easy and rewarding to run up the national debt. All Jeb has to do is pretty much let the nation run its course, and by the end of his eight years, he'll have in his belt-notch the most spectacular failure of all, giving the Bush family a rock-solid reason to be proud.

On Leading the Messed-Up State of Florida

———— ⌀⅂⌐ ————

The state of Florida is not a great state. Not like Texas. In fact, I believe Florida is a pretty messed-up state, to be honest with you. Most of the state is under water, and was for many generations through time nothing more than a swamp filled with terrifying man-eating reptiles. I do not understand why anyone would want to call such a place home, much less the elderly—a great majority of whom migrate to the state in their dying years.

The great and noble Seminole Indians proudly called the state home, but not by choice. It is my understanding that the only reason they lived there was that they had been unable to stake a claim in a more desirable region, such as the Houston, Texas, area. Still, centuries of surviving attacks from water snakes and malaria-ridden mosquitoes in this awful swampland caused these Indians to emerge as a resilient people, capable of amassing many victories when they became the great football team of Florida State University.

But it is worth noting that civilization brought more to the muck and slush of Florida than just a fine football team. It also brought many great diseases, which wiped out most of the native populations in Florida, making way for a stinky cement and asphalt paradise of golf courses, attractive billboard signs, and countless reputable gentlemen's clubs.

But the most important thing civilization brought to Florida was dry land. In one of history's greatest feats of engineering, the builders of the state of Florida created a raised bed of peat moss and earth and suspended it over the swamp. This miraculous, bright green solid ground—a catwalk, essentially, that covers millions of square miles and upon which Florida's residents and visitors walk, run, and even drive—has allowed the state to build something resembling a viable economy and adequate, though hardly vibrant, political life.

Somehow the raisers of the state have also managed to suspend the golf courses atop the swamp so that the golfers do not even notice the sagging and drooping land beneath their feet. Speaking as someone who has played a great deal of golf in Florida, I can attest to this marvel of man's accomplishments on this Earth. It is a testament to the great workmanship of the Seminole tribesmen who raised these golf courses using tomahawk-carved Pigmy Date Palm trees as hoists and steadied them with crude rope made from alligator hide and guar gum. Knowing these facts, it is a wonder that large swaths of these golf courses do not become giant Floridian sinkholes more often.

Not much happened in Florida in the intervening years, post-land-raising, save for the establishment of an amusement park by the great Ward Disney, who was a renowned hirer of doodlers. Evidently he built a successful business in Orlando flinging youngsters this way and that, and offering guided tours through the great castle of cardboard that he erected atop the bog. Even today personalized caps with two circles atop them are available from roadside fruit stands as nostalgic rememberings of this amusing business park, which I believe went out of business in the 1970s due to the advent of the far more popular youth activity of roller rinks.

Our great rocket ships to the moon were launched from Florida because of the soft landing provided by the swampland. In the event any of the rockets ever malfunctioned and fell over during takeoff, the rocket blasterers of NASA hoped that any rocket so discharged would be salvageable after a simple spraying, draining, and cleaning out of all the wet saw-grass gunk and snakes from the rocket's inner workings. This would be more efficient, they reasoned, than trying to put a rocket back together after falling into pieces on solid ground. The inhospitable Florida environment also made training for our astronauts much easier. Sloshing through the Everglades in a full-body space suit proved to be excellent training for walking in the desolate vacuum of outer space, and the frequent encounters with alligators prepared our early astronauts for any predatory moon-beasts they may encounter on the lunar surface.

After this long period of desolation and uneventfulness, there came a great leader to the state of Florida, one who, with his great vision of a lower tax on corporations and a "choose life" license plate, would inspire the people of this strange wetland to emerge from the slime and reach a higher purpose. He would lead the people of Florida to a few years of prosperity for everyone from the hardworking owners of golf clubs, to the successful owners of gentlemen's clubs, all the way down to the humble venture-capital investors and entrepreneurs, all of whom labor in pastel pink or blue buildings, topped with billboards advertising the gentlemen's clubs and golf courses.

The name of this near-mythical figure was Jeb Bush.

Mythical figure, you say? I said the same thing. To think that my brother could do the fantastical things I am about to tell you about is antithetical to all the things I believe about my fatheaded kid brother.

Jeb debuted on the world stage as a great hero of Florida when he came to the aid of a poor woman named Terri Schiavo. The woman was near death in a Florida swamp, fighting for her life after an attack from a deadly swap-frog. She was in a coma. Her family and her brave Seminole guides attempted to carry her out of the swap, but they could not, and for years she lay hovering near death. Jeb hacked his way through the heavy swamp grass with a machete from a palm branch and half an alligator jaw, which he tore from the brute with his own hands. Sweating, exhausted, and his shirt torn exposing his formidable belly, he emerged at Terri's side and lifted her up, carrying her to the safety of a nearby hospital, where they had the technology to keep her alive indefinitely. Terri Schiavo's family and those keeping vigil at her side in the swamp wept and prayed. They thanked the Good Lord for sending this heroic blubber-butt to deliver Terri Schiavo from death.

Eventually she did die, but Jeb did everything in his power to keep her hooked up to those machines. It was a sad loss for him, and for the machines, who worked so hard.

Jeb also heard the anguished cries of the people of Florida who wanted to bring offshore drilling to the state. They longed for someone brave enough to stand up to the powerful coral-reef interests. He fought hard to bring the people this much-needed drilling, and continues to put his efforts into this higher cause to this day.

Jeb is a fighter. That is why he championed the "stand your ground" law, an excellent law that allowed people to shoot other people. This is what the state of Florida needed.

Also lost in the great history of Florida is the fact that Jeb brought oranges to the sunshine state. Before Jeb arrived, the sweetest fruit crop of the locals was turnips, which I do not believe are even classified as a fruit, but rather a tuber. At that time, scurvy was routing the middle class of Florida.

At one time, the Bushes were one of the few lucky families that could afford oranges. Jeb would have oranges flown in fresh every day from an orange grove in California. But in his goodness and magnanimity as a leader, he realized regular folks might also like oranges.

However, the chartered FedEx jet bringing Jeb his morning orange juice every day—while a justifiable expense—only had room for one person's oranges.

How would the great hero of Florida solve this daunting problem for his people?

His thinking was if we could harvest oil without having to search for the oil wells in the wild, he could do the same with oranges. He first tried drilling for oranges off the Florida coast, hoping where oil could not be found, oranges would be brought forth. This effort failed to produce oranges. He next decided to plant many orange trees in one place. He bought a plot of land, and started seeding it with seeds left over from his breakfast slice of orange every morning.

He had what they call an "orange thumb," because every one of those seeds took root. And soon he had a field of orange trees the size of a Texas oil field. It took a few years before the field bore fruit, but ultimately he was able to harvest bushels of fruit. The funny thing is, the orange farm also produced oil, so it was doubly profitable for him and his family.

His endeavor a great success, he started to travel the state with a bag of orange seeds, visiting landowners all over and planting seeds on their land whether they wanted them or not. Orange fields sprang up from Orlando to whatever the southernmost place in Florida is. Maybe it is Pensacola, because that is another city in Florida that I can think of. And orange juice started to flow bountifully from the state, via the orange-grove pipelines that took it all over to a juice-parched nation. These pipelines were shared with oil companies, but a great effort was made to clean the pipes so that no oil would get into the orange juice, and perhaps just as importantly, so that no orange juice would get in the oil.

Supermarkets in places like North Dakota, Maine, and Idaho were able to sell oranges and orange juice to the poor at a price they could somewhat afford. Soon, kids were having a full glass of juice every morning, unheard of mere years before.

The scurvy epidemic began to recede. People everywhere wondered who this magical orange seeder was. Jeb's name became synonymous with vitamin C. His face is still on one of the brands of vitamin C sold in Florida health food stores, I believe.

Now, understand that I myself still find it hard to believe that Jeb could accomplish all of this. To me he'll always be my dopey little brother who smells like an orange rind. But I do respect, to an extent, his contributions to the strange state of Florida.

Aside from all of his other good works in Florida, our great nation will forever be in Jeb's debt for one important act: providing the public service of counting all of those ballots with the hanging chads, resulting in the 537 votes that made me the President of the United States in 2000. Thanks, Jeb!

Jeb: Master of the "E-Mail"

———— ∽ ————

There is a type of mail that does not get delivered by postal service employees. It is a type of mail that does not go in an envelope. It does not require a stamp. It does not require the correct zip code. You do not have to lick it to seal it, or use a letter opener to open it. In fact, you don't even have to wait for it to arrive.

What kind of an impossible, future-time letter am I talking about? I am talking about the "e-letter." It is a type of letter that is written—rather, typed!—on a computer, and then, by a wondrous technology understood by a select few, the letter is "electronic-mailed" to a recipient at another computer. This computer may not even be in the same house!

If you have not heard of these miracle letters, let me explain them to you. I am in a unique position to do so, since, as a former US President who served as our nation's commander in chief in a time of war, I have been privy to super-advanced communications technologies available only to world leaders and titans of business, to whom the delay of even one day can mean the difference between suffering a loss of a life, or worse, losing millions of dollars. Here is the amazing story of my first receipt of one of these "e-mail letters":

It was at a time when the future had arrived, and new tools were available to those in high command that were undreamed of in prior times. The year was 2003. I was seated in the War Room of the White House. The leading-edge forms of communication tools were at my fingertips, and I was surrounded by accomplished generals and admirals who were trained to use them in order to fulfill important missions in wartime. This was a time when pen and paper, telegraph, even the bullhorn were not enough to meet the needs of the day. As I sat in front of this "e-mailing" screen, troops were on the ground in Iraq. A major ground offensive was about to be launched against the enemy in Baghdad to capture Iraq dictator Saddam Hussein. The commanding general in the field, Tommy Franks, needed the okay to give the order to his fighting men and women. He needed to speak to his commander in chief (me). But the infrastructure of Iraq was in shambles, therefore the phone lines were down. There was not a reliable cell-phone connection, either. Some of my advisors and the Joint Chiefs, who were at my side in Washington, suggested we use the new and untested mode of communicating known as "e-writing."

Here's how it worked. I typed the message into a computer in the Situation Room. Some other men in the room pressed some buttons on the computer for me. Then, within minutes, that message appeared on a computer in General Franks's command tent, which he was then able to "print out" on paper to read. We had successfully broken the "e-barrier" in mail. And many lives were saved that day.

Now, I understand that not every person has access to the level of technology afforded a commander of modern wartimes, who has the aid of teams of men and accomplished generals required to tell him how to push the necessary buttons to send out an "e-message" like this, and the mere idea of communicating in a way that seems centuries beyond our everyday lives is probably difficult for you, the average reader of this book, to comprehend. However, there are some who do understand these machines form tomorrow. Some have learned about this "e-computing" in special classes or through years of diligent study of books written about computers—maybe even *by* computers. These people are—believe it or not—able to send and receive the "e-computerized letters" nearly every day, from their homes or workplaces.

One of those technical super-brains is Jeb Bush.

Jeb was known when he was Governor of Florida as the "e-Governor" because of his mastery of sending special "e-notes" to average citizens of his state when they would write to him. I'm not certain if these poor citizens could make any sense of these gobbledegook messages from their Governor when they received them, since surely not every one of them owned the required "e-constructing computer" that was calibrated for receiving such mail on the other end. But for those who did, the future had arrived—and they were able to carry on a discourse with their Governor solely though the "e-wires" connected by electricity to "e-envelopes."

Come to think of it, I doubt Jeb carried on any kind of meaningful discourse with citizens. Surely, it was strictly a one-way conduit of information, in which citizens wrote to Jeb, then he sent them a terse reply, fully satisfying whatever query or issue they had raised. Any follow-up communication beyond that was surely only possible though the payment of a burdensome surcharge.

Nonetheless, Jeb conducted all manner of state business through these "talking-e" contraptions. He wished married couples well upon their being issued a marriage license. He congratulated motorists when they passed their driver's license tests. When people asked complicated questions about controversial topics, Jeb would send them a note making them aware of his firm position on the policy, always careful to never be open to any kind of argument made by the citizen.

It is a wonder how Jeb was able to conduct affairs of state through such unfathomed modern technology. I look on it in awe. The speed of all of these "e-mailers" going in and out of computers with the sound of electricity begs the question, didn't some of the computers break? How could anyone find these "g-notes" when they were moving so fast? Were crack teams of electricians with special training brought in to fortify all of the electrical boards and connectors in the state in order to clear the way for these "electro-message-carriers" to get through? How did people open old-fashioned letters when they had been "digilized" right in their hands with a sudden flash of bright green light?

These and many more questions will have to remain in the mists of knowledge, where all the impossible questions go. For no one can possibly reckon all of these things which move as fast as a computer-brain.

The larger question is, how does this "electronic-L" work?

To understand this new type of postal service, one must first understand the computers that make it possible.

Computers are great machines that can think ten or even twenty times faster than a human being. By now, hundreds of people own their own computers and their own "virtual electricity." These "thinking i-boxes" calculate numbers and play chess and do other things which normal humans cannot do, and must be plugged into a wall outlet. This is important, I have learned.

Once powered, the computer screen lights up, and there you will find instructions for how to "compute" the mails. Typically these instructions involve typing many numbers and letters into the computer using the "key-board," which is also where the source-letters sent through the "e-post" are located.

So how do the letters in the box get to where they're going? Here's where things get complicated. Because in order to understand these complex concepts further, you must know about "the Internets."

What are "the Internets"?

No one knows for sure. I first introduced many Americans to the concept during my 2000 debate with Vice President Al Gore, who once claimed to have contributed some of the parts necessary to weave these "nets" out of calculators. But this is in dispute. Ted Stevens helped the world understand that the Internets stream tubes to us with free movies. It truly is remarkable technology, based essentially on very small cylinders.

I have experience working with my own Internet. When someone Internets me an "AOL," I receive that Internet on my computer, and then it is a "virtual v-letter." Others may have had this experience as well with their own "chips."

But how does it all work?

"The Webs" come from mechanical circuits built by the minds of science that are suspended in the clouds above our planet, tied together with powerful and specially spun inter-i-twine. Originally constructed to guide missiles to destroy the "Inter-web," an adjunct to the Internet used by China for "linking" and certain types of weaponized "e-clicks," these "Interwebbing-cyberspaces" now serve a peaceful purpose.

These computer-Internets are connected to the ground units in homes and offices using special invisible aero-wires. The ground units use boiled electricity water inside the computer screens to "process-link" stored net-files such as pictures of cats or articles about the television program *Star Trek*. No one knows how computers store information such as this, but the leading thinkers believe they are carried on light beams by microscopic Internet centaur-like creatures who ride back and forth on neutron lasers that make a *"pacheew"* space-rifle type of sound. They do this while howling an eerie, otherworldly cry for help, since carrying all of these "bites" of information is very painful to them, despite their tough half-human, half-equestrian hides. Others say they ride inside virtu-pipes that carry them to "online" rooms where they can "social."

Keep in mind all of this happens inside a single computer key, smaller than the human eye can perceive. The point is, all anyone really knows is that it works, most of the time. When it is plugged in.

If you speed up the process, and send some of these cloud-beams through streaming-wires, the process is increased to what's known as "broadband net." This is where Internets increase to ten, thirty, or even 4G, and they have enough cyber-power to send-click not only hyperlinking but also "serve" in a "download" format as well.

Technician lingo aside, this all poses an ethical question. Will we someday all use this "net," and give up the handwritten letters we now drop in mail-teleportation boxes on our virtual street corners?

Well, I for one hope we never do away with good old letters. If we did, how would my dear old dad communicate with me? But the future is changing, and times are coming. And there is no telling what these cyber-things will offer up next. Maybe we will be able to send instructional manuals or recipes over the cloud-nets. The mind reels with such configurationings!

But I am not the one to predict such things. If you truly want to understand all about this, you should talk to Jeb, because he is the expert. He's the one everyone in my family calls when our digi-net m-mails get caught in the super-outlook-highway.

The Foolproof Method by Which the Republican Party Selects a Nominee

———⌁———

The great founders of our nation crafted an ingenious system for electing Presidents. It may not be perfect, but it is certainly the best system in the world. (USA is, after all, number one.) How do the most suitable contenders emerge from amongst our vast land? How are they vetted, and how do they demonstrate their strength, will, and grace under pressure that will be necessary when sitting in the highest command desk? And when and how do the American people get to make their small contribution to the final decision?

Before we can determinate if Jeb Bush is worthy to lead our country, it would be appropriate to go through the detailed step-by-step procedure that the GOP uses to select a candidate. Can Jeb pass their mustard? We shall see.

It all starts with the Republican Committee. Before candidates are even announced, a thorough filtering process weeds out any names of candidates that are too foreign-seeming, too terroristy, or even one that just sounds wrong. Nobody wants a President with a wrong name, like Lipshitz, Dunderheimer, or Boner. If a candidate has a dumb name like one of these fine folks, it is up to that candidate to legally change it or otherwise normify it prior to seeking the Republican nomination. Or they are welcome to seek the nomination of some other party. The Farm-Labor Party, for example, would likely be pleased to nominate a qualified candidate named Stanley Nutjob.

After the critical name-vetting step, Republican Committee operatives sneak into the homes of candidates and read their private diaries, to see if they have expressed a heartfelt wish to be President. If there is a short passage in the diary, or perhaps even a vision board or colorful collage with cutouts and hand-drawn hearts all pointing to a dream of being in the White House, we know that we have the right man. The diary readings are kept strictly confidential, and only leaked to the press if the candidate one day turns on the Republican Party and needs to be brought down through a humiliating scandal.

After the prospective candidate is given qualified approval by the Republican Committee, he then moves onto his own Presidential Exploratory Committee. This is an important step that invites learned men of letters—professors, philosophers, wise men, and clergy—to explore the potential candidate's mental, physical, and spiritual fitness to endure the rigors of the Oval Office.

The Exploratory Committee, appropriately, explores the country, meeting and interacting with common folk, accepting shelter each night from those they meet on their journey. They sleep on straw beds in rustic barns, find shelter in remote inns or on the stoops of kindly Samaritans. There they describe the candidate to the local people to gain an understanding of the issues that are most important to these regular Americans. Committee members take on some light chores in the voters' barns in order to earn their keep, and otherwise become active participants in the struggles these commoners face in their daily lives. A committee member might deliver a calf, slaughter

a pig for breakfast, or put down a beloved dog who has sadly con-
tracted the Mange, or the Chronic Moaning. They hold and comfort
the family's young children while they lovingly place the shotgun
to the animal's head, cover it with a towel, then do what must be
done. There may be tears, but everyone's life is changed by the experience, and important lessons are learned.

When it is time to move on, some of the voters' children won't
want to see these kindly strangers go, but go they must. There are
more voters to meet and interact with, in order to explore their candidate's suitability for higher office.

If one of these regular voters comes to value the committee's candidate, that voter's name is inscribed in the official leather-bound
Exploratory Committee Scroll. Then the Exploratory Committee
will roll up the scroll and disappear into the sunset, walking down
a lonely road, perhaps with sad piano music playing, only to deeply
impact another life next week.

Once thirty million names are written in the scroll, the candidate
passes this initial phase of the nomination process, and moves onto
the next.

At this juncture, a band of specially appointed dwarf warriors
must meet in the home of the hopeful nominee and sing a soothing
thirteen-hour chant of electoral-vote blessings before the journey of
the candidate to statesmanhoodship can begin.

Accompanied by the dwarves and perhaps a kindly wizard, the
candidate makes it official and announces his candidacy. He must do
this from the top of Mount McKinley for all the nation to hear. There
is a special press-briefing room and attached bullhorn atop the great
mountain for this express purpose.

The next phase is that the candidate must woo the delegates. Delegates are dedicated believers who live high above the towns in dark

caves. They rule over the towns of our country with their powerful delegating sticks, and wield great power over the man who will be our next leader, for it is they who are entrusted to make the journey to Minneapolis, Denver, or wherever the party's convention will be held, to cast the critical votes needed for the candidate to receive the Republican Party's nomination.

To meet the delegates, the candidate himself must travel by rickshaw to every state and charm the delegates of every province in person. The candidate must ride his rickshaw up the craggy rocks outside of the villages until the road is too rough to go any further. Then he must hike up to the delegate cave alone—with no guide, and often under extreme duress, carrying a heavy pack without the aid of a mule—and offer tribute to the delegate. A succulent cut of fresh meat, a freshly tanned hide, or a local merchant gift card are all suitable bestowals.

Once the delegates of all fifty states are all sufficiently wooed, the candidate moves on to the next difficult challenge.

I should add at some point in here that it is also important that the candidate amass hundreds of million dollars from wealthy donors who in no way influence the process.

The next step is a rigorous training period, where experts in all manner of public office and current affairs of state use flash cards to drill the candidate with difficult questions such as, "How many branches of the federal government are truly needed?" and "Senegal is a nation in what African country?" Impressively, a candidate who goes through this grueling training receives the equivalent of a fourth-grade education in just a few days.

After the flash cards, a standardized test must be taken. The candidate must receive a passing grade on the RSTAT, which determines basic knowledge of the Republican national platform, and only a score over eight-five secures eligibility for the Republican nominee. Candidates can opt out of the RSTAT if they have scored over forty on the GOPT, or over ninety on the POTUSEE or POTUS-SAT, which determine advanced understanding of not only Republican policies, but also national government and the names of world leaders.

Older candidates can be grandfathered in without taking any of the standardized tests as long as at some point they have passed either the PLEE or the FLARP.

Copies of these tests must be ordered from the testing authority and taken at an authorized testing facility, where they are sealed with a wax signet of the candidate. The tests must be sealed by the candidate in an envelope 6⅛ inches tall, 12 inches long, affixed with exactly three times first-class postage and mailed to the home address of political operative Frank Luntz. This is a tricky requirement designed to test the candidate's attention to detail. Many a candidate has been thrown off by this simple little requirement. William H. Seward, it is rumored, sent in his tests in an envelope only 6¹⁄₂ inches tall, and therefore failed to secure the party's nomination in 1860, resulting in a lifetime of bitter regret in which he wandered the country in search of the proper-sized envelope. But he had been passed over by history, and by mailing supplies, for all times.

The next challenge, which is the most fierce gauntlet the candidate must endure, is a crucible of words wielded by powerful threshold guardians known as "reporters." Reporters are silver-tongued adversaries who ambush a candidate and try to trick him into saying something that will cause voters to lose confidence in him, or something that will make him look foolish. These devilish journalists will ask any question they believe will trip up the candidate, and continue to ask the question even when ignored, until they achieve their dastardly goal of confusing and flustering the candidate. A candidate must remain firm and calm, for if he answers the reporters' questions, he may be caught in one of their fiendish traps.

It is hoped that in the future we will find a way to remove reporters from the process, but for that to happen, laws must be changed. Until that sweet day, every prospective candidate must face their wrath.

What makes this reporter gauntlet even more challenging is that whenever the candidate speaks to reporters, he must stand on a bed of burning coals during the conversation. After, he must personally defeat each one of the press corps in mortal combat. This is typically very easy because many of the press corps are old, out of shape, or relatively sedentary. However, candidates pray they do not face the likes of Anderson Cooper, Wolf Blitzer, or Larry King, for they are undefeated in their gauntlet guarding.

Once these adversaries are dispatched, the candidate must hoist a boiling cauldron out of the way of a secret portal, thus emblazoning on his forearms for the rest of his natural days the marks of a successful Republican presidential candidate. Look closely at the pale inner arms of candidates when you next see them stumping, and you might see the elephant-ear-shaped scars left by this trial.

The candidate must then wander through the cold, wintery wilderness alone, without shoes on his feet. For three days and nights he must search his soul to find his true purpose for seeking the office.

Finally, the convention is held. This is where the candidate speaks to the nation in a large auditorium, and paper flags with the names of states are counted aloud to determine if the candidate has enough votes to be a grand marshal in the party parade. There is much confetti and many balloons as part of this process. This is where the final decision is made. All the factors are considered by all the delegates, and they throw millions of tiny pieces of paper into the air. These papers are mixed with balloons to distract the voters at home, who are enamored with balloons. But it is these papers that hold the key.

Once all of these papers have fallen to the ground, the delegates painstakingly collect them in their straw hats, and then count them. The candidate with the most votes wins the nomination.

At the end of the paper-counting, there is that big parade and ice-cream social in the town square to celebrate the grand-marshal candidate.

It's that simple.

Jeb has a good chance to come out on top of this intense winnowing process, but what kind of a President would he be if he won the election? That is what we must determine next.

What a President Jeb Will Do for Our Family—I Mean, Country

———— ✧ ————

The first thing a sitting President must do is select a top-notch staff. I'm proud to say many honored public servants from my administration are being tapped by Jeb to reclaim their old roles: Attorney General Alberto Gonzales; Harriet Miers, who, after some night classes in Constitutional Law, is now ready to take her rightful seat on the Supreme Court; our brother Neil, whose extensive savings and loan experience in the 1980s makes him an excellent economic advisor. "Brownie" is excited to get to work getting FEMA whipped back out of shape. There are many others. Jeb would be well served—heck, I'll even say he *needs*—the experienced hand of these veteran White Housers to balance out his own inexperience and first-timitude.

Perhaps the most important member of a President's staff is his right-hand man, his Vice President. I do not know who Jeb will finally select for this important role. I do not even know who Jeb will select to advise him on who to select as Vice President, or who to select to advise him on the best advisor to help advise him on who to select for this advisor, or even who to advise him on advising him on how to advise him to find an advisor who can advise advisors with the best advice-giving capabilities. But I'm sure whoever it is will be the best qualified and most intensely vetted of all. I do know that one of our history's great public servants, Dick Cheney, has already left several voice mail messages for Jeb volunteering to head up a vice presidential search committee, a role he capably played when I was running for President. I am confident that Dick Cheney will again select the best man for the job.

Also among the first priorities is to select close advisors and aides. Jeb already has many such individuals on his campaign staff, so he has already thoroughly vetted some of these great minds. Chief among them, of course, is me. I play a significant role behind the scenes as a presidential-contender advisor, making sure that Jeb stays on the straight and arrow. My specialty in this regard is that I am his point man on the Middle East, an area of the world where I know a thing or two, having fought two or perhaps three wars there. I also know the local language spoken by most of the US soldiers stationed in the region. And I know their customs, having flown in specially to serve them a turkey on Thanksgiving that one time.

Of course now, with the benefit of both hindsight and experience, I bring a new and wiser perspective to the running of a country—I bring an artist's perspective. And through the medium of art, I can advise Jeb in a way other experts and knowledge-makers cannot. I will ask probing questions that most, unless they have extensive experience painting, would never think to ask. Should a President lead with bold reds and vibrant blues, or with a more subdued, hazy yellow or Chamoisee? Where should the eye be directed in the "tableau" of the nation's leadership?

Further, my experience as a painter has many other potential benefits to Jeb, should he turn to me for counsel. I am at Jeb's disposal to be on hand to paint beautiful images to present at his presidential press conferences. I would unveil paintings that convey all the information he needs to communicate to an anticipatory press corps. He would not have to say a word, because the painting, which as we all know is worth a thousand words, would do his speaking for him. I could paint a call to war. I could paint a heartfelt response to a national tragedy. I look forward to the possibility of responding to each individual question from the White House press corps. When a reporter from, say, the *Washington Post*, asks Jeb a question about, say, why we are sending drones to bomb inside the Syrian border, I would paint a striking canvas to illustrate his response. Instead of responding, Jeb would gesture to me, and I would begin painting. Some patience on the part of the press corpser may be required, as it often takes me several days to complete a painting. Even when I think a painting is done, sometimes I find it necessary to sleep on it for a few more days to make sure it truly represents the thoughts and feelings I mean to express. I don't think Jeb and the press corps will mind waiting. Perhaps Jeb's press secretary could recommend that the press corps bring sleeping bags to accommodate this new method of conducting press briefings.

In the end, the information from the painting will be so comprehensive, and so satisfying, not only on an informational level, but on an emotional level as well, that I believe both the press corps and the public at large will embrace the new approach. Art has the power to enlighten, which would turn press conferences into a wonderful opportunity not only for the press to get vital information from the executive branch, but to learn about themselves as well.

After selecting advisors, staffs, and aides, Jeb will get to work making our country greater. He will communicate his forward-looking platform (which, as I understand it, is the same as the

Republican Party platform written in 1992). Chief among the issues on his platform will be immigration. Jeb's view on the immigration issue and our border with Mexico is murky, given the fact that he learned the local language in order to convince everyone that he had a beautiful girlfriend there. He has even called himself "the first Hispanic candidate" for President. I am certain he will figure out a way to skillfully un-explain that remark when the time is right. For now, he will remain tough on immigration, but I am uncertain as of this writing what skillful words and phrases he and his people will concoct in order to achieve this daunting feat.

In our private talks, Jeb has expressed a great love for the people south of our border, and he has laid out a vengeful vision for how to close off that border to everyone except his make-believe bride. He dreams of constructing a twenty-foot-high electrical fence with an alligator-filled moat on our side. And with electric eels. There'll be one way in and out, with a formidable electric gate that goes up and down, letting in only the people he wants. The whole apparatus will be electric. Jeb understands the power of electricity.

But he will not stop with our Mexican border.

On the issue of our northern border, Jeb's views are clear. Too often our economy struggles under the weight of illegals who yearn to escape from the socialized health insurance and gun-controlling tyranny of Canada. They are pained by the environmental legislation that prevents folks of good conscience from freely exercising their right to dump chemicals and mining waste in the rivers and streams of Canada. They yearn for the freedom we have in this country to pollute the air, water, and land as God intended. They yearn for liberty. Our hearts can go out to these poor people, but we cannot help them. They come here to work for low wages in the entertainment industry as television hosts and comedy celebrities. It is upsetting when we hear of companies like NBC who employ Canadians like Lorne Michaels, Dan Aykroyd, and others, paying them "off the books." They are taking jobs away from hardworking American comedians.

Jeb is firm on our need to secure the northern border. He supports the building of a two-hundred-mile snow-wall to block out these illegals from the north. Giant refrigeration units will keep this wall frozen year-round. Border agents armed with cups of water to ensure the wall stays slick and frozen will guard the wall, wearing only animal skins and armed with sharp spears.

A discussion of Jeb's homeland security priorities would not be complete without a thorough examination of his approach to Terror.

Terror is a difficult issue for any President to fight. But Jeb will not be working alone. Great leaders have already laid the ground-land for a successful strategizery against those who would harm our nation with the tools of Terror. My father, first and foremost, laid the foundation with the Gulf War. I put up the studs and the beams with Operation Dessert Storm. Jeb will finish the house, paint it, and put nice light fixtures in there. This complicated, what they call "analogy," refers to the good work we have done to fight the extremists. My father batted at the hornet's nest in Iraq, which left us with an even more stable Middle East, bringing life to the new enemy of Al-Qaeda. I smoked them out of their holes, which led to the honing of the even more powerful adversary, known as ISIS. Jeb will really bring the fight to the Terrorists.

Jeb knows that the tougher the enemy, the tougher the America. We can only be as strong as our opponent, something he learned from the various thrashings I gave him growing up. So, Jeb will help bring about an as yet unimaginably powerful Terror adversary, a group even more powerful than ISIS, with new and more calculating

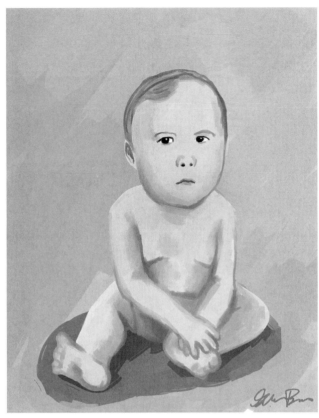

This is what Jeb looked like as a baby—a doughy-faced blob that didn't have much of any substance to say. He hasn't changed a bit.

Here is one of my first paintings, a "still life" of a bowl of fruit. If you look closely, you can make out the likeness of Jeb in one of the apples. At least I can. That is how I justify this painting's inclusion in this book.

In this important painting, I captured the vision-dream that came to me as a young boy, propelling me on a life-changing quest to shape Jeb's heart into that of a presidenting contender.

Jeb tending to his orange grove in Florida. Notice all the color orange in this painting. Representing oranges. Can't see the orange? That's because color printing is much more expensive than black and white, and the good folks at the book publishing company have opted to save a few bucks and destroy my art. My heart hangs heavy for your loss.

I painted this picture of Jeb's spirit animal, the mighty turtle. I was suddenly inspired to create this one after drinking some especially strong tea. This tiny reptilian beast is suggestive of supernatural powers and the occult. And it kind of looks like Jeb!

Here is an "action painting" of Jeb catching a Frisbee I threw to him at the beach. This is an astounding talent he has that not too many people know about.

This is a painting of my former workplace, and, if he is deemed worthy, Jeb's next workplace as well. There is much white, of course, but I also imbued it with broad brushstrokes and deep blacks, which signify war, shock, and awe.

Kittens!

Here I have painted Jeb participating in the GOP pie-eating contest. There really isn't a GOP pie-eating contest, but it might be fun for me and the nation at large to think of Jeb doing that, with pie all over his face.

Part of being a presidential candidate is accepting donations from engaged, civic-minded voters. Here Jeb is accepting the mattress savings of a kindly old corporation from Houston, Texas.

I call this painting Jebraham Lincoln. I created it in the hopes this art would replace all the dusty old paintings of Abraham Lincoln that presently clutter up the White House.

Here is Jeb going to work on his first day.

Jeb takes a lot of pictures of himself, so here is, appropriately, a picture of him taking a picture! It is what they call "self-referensorial" art.

This is Jeb chopping down the ISIS sign, like he will do if he's President. This painting uses "symbolism," in which the sign symbolizes ISIS, and, more broadly, Terror. More subtly, the bright shiny axe blade represents the sharp minds behind our country's anti-Terror policies.

Jeb participating in a Virtual Presidential Debate, preparing for his candidatehood. I believe this is how they will do debates in the future, and perhaps even today. The bold angle of this painting illustrates that Jeb is winning.

A beautiful likeness of three generations of Bush Presidents.

leaders, who will pursue unthinkably horrible tortures of captive enemies. And their names will be even newer, more unfathomable acronyms, using the scariest letters in our alphabet.

In response, Jeb will turn up the heat on the Terrorists, because this is the only way we can win against them. With hotter carpet-bombs. With louder gunneries. Keep the heat above the burning point of these Terror-fighters. Then these next-generation Terrorists will respond with even more devastating attacks on the US that will only make us tougher. Someday it is possible that an enemy of the US will drop a nuclear bomb on an American target. Then we'll really get 'em.

In relation to this goal, Jeb will commit to spending upwards of 90 percent of the federal budget on defense: nuclear bombs, nuclear subs, battleships, fighter jets, and drones—all the kinds of modern machines of warfare that have so far proven effective in our fight against small, agile groups of insurgents who live in caves and are often armed with nothing more than a knife. Jeb will do it right—and he will spend as much money as possible on weapons systems that can go up against those very sharp knives.

Jeb will also inspire more young people to join the fight, serving their country proudly by becoming decorated and highly paid Halliburton contractors in the fight against the ISISers. Jeb knows how important these patriotic young recruits are, and he will personally visit our high schools and officer training schools to encourage our best and brightest kids to send their résumés to Kellogg Brown & Root, Blackwater, and the other brave companies who are defending our nation and fighting the good fight.

What else will Jeb do besides war? Let me think. Well, Jeb will bring many other fresh new ideas to revitalize our nation's economy, for one thing. He will bring it back to the boom years of 2007 to 2008.

One exciting concept Jeb will implement is the "preemptive bailout." Before there's a tragedy, like the collapse of a major bank, for example, Jeb will convince Congress to appropriate trillions of dollars and give it to the wealthiest citizens, largest banks, and credit card companies. This forward-thinking strategy will stop financial collapses before they happen.

As I chaptered before, Jeb believes in the "e's." Of course those "e's" refer to the web-power. Another vital "e" Jeb will focus on as President is e-ducation. To this end, Jeb will encourage the use of computers in teaching our kids, who have yet to learn what computers are.

Beyond that, Jeb will streamline the No Child Left Behind Act. It will be lean, and turbocharged under a Jeb Bush administration. It will send kids through school in half the time. Many will graduate high school and be ready for the workforce by the time they are nine years old. Our growing economy needs these energetic young entrepreneurs. Jeb hasn't thought of a name for it yet, but it'll probably be something like the "Every Children Jump Ahead Act," or the "Get 'em Through Quick Act."

Jeb will make other improvements to the No Child Left Behind Law, or whatever we're going to call it. For one, he will update it so it doesn't leave so many children behind. It's true there were some stragglers. Not every student worked hard enough, and some bad apples had to be thrown under the bus. They were in the way of a great law, is the problem. Jeb will find those kids, who are all grown up now and living in halfway houses, and he will see to it that they are put into our nation's finest prisons. There they will have access to a hot shower, exercise equipment, and perhaps a magazine or two. Through these old issues of *In Touch* or *Shape*, these sad, once-young people will rediscover the joy of reading, and become productive members of their prison community.

Some believe our great nation has become more tense between the racial lines, what with folks of color perceiving that white law enforcement officers are getting off scot-free after unfairly targeting them for random, multiple-shooting deaths. I don't know what the heck they're taking about. But whatever the case, it is important we have a President who understands the races and who will bridge the racial devoid. Jeb believes those poor white officers deserve to be treated like everyone else, and he will fight for them, because, like the protesters say, the lives of our white officers matter, too.

Jeb has a great love for our races. He loves the black folks. He loves the Mexicans. He will unflinchingly shake hands with persons of any race briefly while on the campaign trail. Even of the GLTB race. Jeb supports all kinds of people, no matter how different, dark, strange, or wrong.

Many people fail to appreciate that the commander in chief job is largely made up of ceremony. And Jeb will be up to the task. He will declare the earwig to be the National Insect. He will declare Coors to be the National Beverage. And he will declare Texas and Florida to be the nation's National States. He will veto any bill that comes across his desk sponsored by a lady senator. He will find lovely *Avengers*-themed curtains for the Oval Office.

Lastly, and perhaps most importantly, Jeb will work hard to eliminate waste and abuse in government. It's one of his great goals to get government out of the way of truly helping people. As a true conservative, Jeb does not believe government is the solution to our problems, he believes it is the problem. There is far too much bureaucracy in Washington, and Congress and the Supreme Court can run things just fine on their own. That's why Jeb's dismantling will start with the executive branch itself. He will strip down the White House to a staff of one—a temp worker in the Philippines. Jeb will outsource the handful of essential functions of the President to that very cost-effective employee, and save the taxpayers millions of dollars.

While these things are just my horse sense of what Jeb will do as President, I feel pretty good about my predilections, and feel confident in advising you may take them as a factual blueprint of the future.

With my guidance, Jeb could accomplish great things in the White House. But is he worthy of the office? Only the final chapter of this book can tell. And me, who dictated it.

Turning Controversies into Jebortunities

—— ✦ ——

The road to Jeb's 45ness is not without its stop-blocks. Many feel that he is not the right candidate for the Republican Party in 2016. These contradictors believe, so I'm told, that while he is a formidable candidate, he will not hold up against some of the many other worthy, honorable, and hardworking contenders who are also seeking the nomination.

While I do not know, as of this writing, how many of those fine folks have cowardly turned tail and dropped out of the race like sobbing schoolgirls, I can confidently predict that there are probably a handful who remain to show Jeb some serious competition.

And this competition will work hard and spend a great deal of time and money attempting to reveal Jeb to be a lesser candidate—a candidate who is not strong enough on some of the foundimational Republican principles. Some may even say he is too liberal to be the nominee.

I intend to address those charges here.

Firstly, we must ask, have any of these other contenders been destined for the nomination in the spirit-dream of a former President? I think that is unlikely.

Secondly, I have no second reason, but it is important that I at least provide one, since I began this sentence with the telling word "secondly."

Thirdly, anyone who would label a Bush a "liberal" does not understand the Bush legacy or our ironclad family beliefs.

It is vital that a Republican candidate for President not be perceived as too off-center in what's called the "general" election, a relatively unimportant part of the process in which the mass public has one day to register their opinion during the years-long campaign. If good sense contradicts voter opinion, certain measures can be taken, and it is always nice to know we have that backup plan. But nonetheless, the candidate would do well to be perceived during this time as a "man of the people." Jeb has always had his eye on the prize, and knows how the perception of him as a strong bipartisan leader will be a key strategy for carrying the day.

Jeb has worked very hard on a multi-decade strategy to appear more "centrist" in order to appeal to "swing" voters. During the past thirty years, Jeb has—quite on purpose—adopted a more liberal stance on certain issues in order to create the illusion that he is a moderate. But this is a temporary strategy. He will strategically change his mind back into his genuine conservative views once elected President. It's very much like the "compassionate conservative" label that worked so well for me to hoodwink voters in 2000.

One of Jeb's policies that everyone is harping on is his view on illegal immigrants. Jeb has stated he believes that these border-jumpers should have a path to citizenship. But if you look closely, he can be seen crossing his fingers behind his back and saying to himself, "But only those with immediate family already in the US, who speak English and have some sort of humorous skill like juggling or burping the national anthem."

I must make one other point about these other candidates for the Republican nomination: While I am not familiar with any of their names, I can say with some degree of confidence that none of them are named "Jeb Bush," which is one advantage that my brother holds, given the fact that this, in fact, happens to be his name.

A candidate's name is a very important element in the nomination process, as I've already parstipulated. And I have yet to hear anyone dismiss Jeb on account of his name. Quite to the contrary, they consider him a major opponent—the "one to beat," because of his excellent name. His last name evokes generations of the Bush family legacy, the illusions of which are purely positive. His first name, while unconventional, is approachable, rural-seeming, and quite excellent, according to the presidential-naming experts. "Jeb" is someone you could have a Paleo-friendly smoothie with. It is also a name you could hang out with at the local watering hole. One thing is sure, you would probably enjoy a good laugh due to the engaging and decidedly homespun stories someone with the name "Jeb" is likely to tell.

But aside from these other, lesser candidates, what other serious controversies does Jeb face in this fight?

Some feel that Jeb has made too many goofs and blunders in the past in order to win enough support to emerge the winner of the master in chief. It's good that these "some," whomever they are, bring up these problems, so that I can address them in this definitive book about Jeb. I intend to give a hard, fair look at these controversies, so that supporters can be comforted to know there is nothing to worry about. And I encourage the "some" to correct me on the facts, if they can. I wish them good luck writing their own book to espouse their opinion. A name is not only important in becoming President, it is also important in book-printing. The name "George W.

Bush" warrants getting a book released. I do not believe the book-buying public will be interested in a book written by "some." And the same goes for the "many" who think differently, aberrantly, or wrongly.

Nonetheless, I am going to get all the controversies out of the way, make sure they are all honestly swept under the rug, and forthrightly sidestepped to the point that they can be forgotten. In the interest of "transparency," which is a new "buzz trend" many in governments are embracing, we will openly shove some of these issues back into the closet where they belong, and everyone will be able to see how we seal them from public view for fifty years.

The first controversy I will address is the fact that Jeb's own mother expressed a clear lack of support for his candidacy.

Our mother's lack of support is easy to understand when one realizes not only her history with the Bush family, but also her character. She is only human, as well as half-ogre. It is her ogre half that one must sympathize with. The ogres are a long-maligned race of Eastern Europe. They came through many trials and hard works, lurking in the caves and the dark woods, subsisting on little more than sticks and grubs. The daughter of an ogre immigrant from the mountainous regions of Catatonia, my mother inherited her hard, ogre-minded utility of purpose. There is no time for the frivolities of love, support, or tenderness in the mind of an ogre, and my mother has had to struggle with that.

More importantly, Mother's ability to hold her drink may well turn into an advantage should Jeb win the highest office. She can drink any warlord under the table. Her liver is an ogre liver, abnormally large and effective at eliminating harsh toxins unfit for human consumption. At certain state dinners, if peace with another nation hangs on the outcome of a hastily assembled drinking contest, my mother could turn out to be Jeb's ace in the hole.

We can expect Jeb to be a wartime President. War is always an important part of any good Presidency. So, in a time of war, I believe strongly that we will need a heartless two-fisted drinking beast like Barbara Bush to be the First Mother.

I have already artipulated that I believe the Bush name is a great strength of Jeb's candidacy. Yet a strange controversy that dogs his campaign is that his chances might be hurt by the Bush name. I do not understand this. The Bushes have twelve years of presidency under their collectual belt. Along with eight years of a vice presidency. What other family can claim these kinds of year-numbers? Not even the Roosevelts have had more non-crippled years in office.

Jeb's own Bush family, meaning his so-called "wife" and "children," is also a model of conservative American values. Thanks to some character-defining misdemeanor convictions, jail time, and rehab, they are a family that a broad section of the American public will be able to relate to.

There are some ludicrous rumors of Jeb's affairing. The accusation goes that Jeb consorted with a former Playboy Bunny. Do the accusers imagine Jeb rendezvousing with this Playboy Bunny, and other glamorous Floridian cocktail waitresses, dancers, and maids, surrounding himself with women of questionable virtue who would abide by his every whim? Nothing could be further from the truth. In fact, the mere idea gives me a good laugh.

I suppose there is a remote possibility that some floozie—a good woman, surely, but I will refer to her here as a floozie for the historical purposes of this book—was at some point attracted to Jeb's status as the Governor of Florida. Power, as they say, is the ultimate

anaphylactic. Perhaps she was a confused twenty-something secretary who worked in the executive office. And I suppose it's possible that at some point Jeb was in close quarters with this floozie,
alone, and she decided to initiate some kind of inappropriate physical
contact.

If that ever happened, I can assure you that Jeb's great ineptitude
with women would have repelled the floozie in question very quickly.
He would have first made her extremely uncomfortable by simply
staring at her, his eyes glazed and half-dead-looking. He would then
have roughly pawed at her like a clumsy brute, possibly even harm-
ing her. Then he would have lurched at her face or neck area with a
drooling gape-jawed attempt at a kiss, assaulting her with his blub-
bering wet lips and leaving her with nothing but cold, desperate slob-
ber dripping down her sternum.

Any floozie would rightly be repulsed by these gestures. She would
immediately think better of her fleeting, unreasoned attraction to this
lummox, and repeatedly strike him with all her strength, screaming,
"Get away from me, you...thing!" and run away shrieking.

Jeb would be confused and frightened by her rejection. He would
hunch over in a corner, howling like a wounded seal.

Neither would ever speak of the incident again.

And that's the most that would ever happen! You can trust me on
that one.

Lastly, I want to address the controversy that Jeb has curried favor
for his shifty-eyed friends by leveraging his powerful family connections. While I agree that it would be scandalous had Jeb tried to
make it on his own without taking full advantage of his father's and
my high positions in society and government, I can assure you that
he did nothing of the kind. He made full use of the executive-level
access he has had for many years, leveraging his own connections,

bringing good fortune to many sketchy businessmen, shady dealers, and international Terrorists.

Looking back on it, there aren't that many controversial things about Jeb. He's kind of like a marshmallow. Kinda white, puffy, with an unassuming, bland character. But fire him up and put some graham crackers and chocolate around him, and you've potentially got presidenting material.

The First 100 Gaffes

———— ✺ ————

Every President makes mistakes. The office-haver is, after all, only human. If Jeb is deemed worthy by me and the findings of this book of being our next Command-Chair sitter, he too will make some mistakes. And they will be doozies, because he is a known bumble-klutz. But as a Bush, Jeb will stand by his mistakes and take pride in them, and never waver from his decisions, no matter how wrong. Jeb is known to have a big mouth, and he will say some stupid things as President. I know it in my heart. And I believe he will follow up these stupid words with stupid actions.

How can I confidently know these future happenings? It's simple. I have been preparing Jeb for this moment in history. For his whole life he has been under my wing. I know him like no other. I know his strengths and weaknesses and where he is blunder-prone. Therefore, I can predict with absolute certainty where Jeb will stumble. I can predict with absolute certainty what some of his biggest mistakes will be both during his campaign and during his Presidencing.

In the run-up to the office, Jeb will stick his foot in his mouth a fair number of times. For example, he will refer to his stand-in bride by the wrong name. He will call her "Columbia," which is a mistake I make frequently. The worst of these name gaffes will be when he calls her "Columbine" while stumping for the rights of gun-shooters.

The newsmakers and "bloggings" will not be able to stop harping on that one, I can assure you.

He will also periodically forget some of the names of his pretend children.

At one fundraising event, or perhaps at an Ohio rally, Jeb will drop either a fork, his camera-phone, or a baby. Perhaps two of these at once, if he is taking a photo of himself with the fork or the baby, or if he is trying to feed a baby a bite of fried chicken with his fork and taking a picture of that. I cannot think of an instance where he would drop all three of these items, unless the fork actually belongs to the baby, but I don't believe that counts as his mistake. However, this will not be the real gaffe. When Jeb bends down to pick up the dropped phone or the dropped infant or the dropped fork, he will fall off a stage and bang his head on a chair, and bleed all over it. Blood will be gushing down the side of his head. The press-writers will immediately nickname him "Bleeding-Head Jeb," and the video of his fall will be repeated on the news for several weeks. The upside result of this instance is that because of this injury he will wear an eye patch for the rest of the campaign, thus gaining ground among eye-patch-wearing voters.

When Jeb is cornered by reporters in the dangerous gauntlet of the press conference, they will trip him up, and make him call forth the name of the President of France, which he will not know, and which he will invent. He will call him "President France Francy-France."

While campaigning in rural Idaho, Jeb will get chatting with a regular citizen at a picturesque diner, and in casual conversation with this voter Jeb will let slip that he is not just running for President, he is running for emperor of the galaxy. "I am playing a larger game of domination over the lowly human race," Jeb will say in a noticeably lower and much scarier voice. Jeb will then reveal his true form to the voter, that of a terrifying insect monster from another dimension. The voter will be so frightened that his heart will seize up and he will fall over dead on the spot.

The media-makers will have a fun time with that gaffe for a few days!

Once in office, Jeb will continue screwing up, and he will waste no time doing so. His first mistake as President will be during the inauguration. As the Chief Justice of the Supreme Court recites the oath of office, Jeb will have a hard time remembering some of the longer lines, and when it's his turn to repeat them, he will get toward the end and kind of stumble, then just sort of make up some things, like, "I will faithfully execute the offenders, facing down the scum of this nation, telling them, 'I will be your worst nightmare.'"

He will make more funny slips of the tongue when he is overseas. When meeting with the royal family in the United Kingdom, he will suddenly bat the Queen of England's crown off the top of her head, mistakenly believing it to be a raccoon or other varmint trying to bite her in the scalp. He will go golfing in Scotland and wear the traditional kilt of his hosts, but he will not tie it properly, and round about the fourth hole, his kilt will fall to the ground and everyone will see Jeb's big white butt.

In Japan, during an intricate and prolonged tea ceremony, Jeb will get real thirsty and knock the small Japanese lady out of the way and gulp down all the sweet, nourishing tea, knocking over the table and causing all the priceless porcelain kettles and teacups to come crashing to the ground. But he'll barely notice. He'll just keep guzzling that fine tea.

One thing I'm quite certain of is that Jeb will let out a large belch when speaking to the NAACP annual meeting. In response to this inappropriate outburst, he will simply slap his belly and note how satisfying his lunch had been.

In a related gaffe, Jeb will call all African-Americans "my nig-gaz," which he will do during a cabinet meeting when he does not realize the sound-recording reporters are there. The pundits will really hound him for this one, not realizing that it is in fact accept-able for Jeb to use such a familiar slang term because he met and even associated with some Blacks while he was Governor of Florida, where there are many.

Another scandal we can expect from a Jeb Bush administration is one involving Columba, his captivating yet makeshift bride. Her great beauty will surely ensnare the heart of more than one foreign dignitary, leading to high drama in the White House. The King of Saudi Arabia, or perhaps Siam, will be in attendance for a state din-ner, and his highness will become entranced by Columba's witty table conversation and beguiling fork use. The entranced dignitary will toss and turn in the Lincoln bedroom that night.

"I must have her!" he will say.

Secret Service will keep the kingly agitant from her, and he will be gravely insulted. He will throw down his bejeweled gauntlet at Jeb's feet, demanding his right to fight him for her love. But the agents will drag him from the scene, the dignitary screaming and crying like an infant. When he returns to his home country, he will plot a military campaign against America to win the heart of Jeb's Latin firecracker. Not since the days of the Trojan War will the heart of a jilted lover so move nations to war. The king of one of these inconsequential coun-tries will do anything to win her love.

All of this will be good for Columba, because it will give her something to do. All First Ladies need a cause, everything from Laura Bush's focus on teaching kids to read to something as different as my mother Barbara Bush's focus on literacy.

Jeb will indeed fight several duels during his tenure. Whether it be an untoward comment about Gopher, the White House ferret, or Jeb's own buffoonery, like accidentally-on-purpose passing wind on a foreign dignitary's face after Jeb has tackled and sat on him, more gloves will be thrown down. Fortunately, the only weapons to duel with at the White House are wooden swords, which hang in the White House Sword Room. But there will be some vicious red welts inflicted. The media will call this barbarism. Jeb's White House will call it justice.

There will also be some ridiculous photos posted on the e-nets. I expect Jeb's seat-crack will most likely be a recurring feature on CNBC.com. Because whenever he bends down to pick something up, tie his shoe, or pet a dog, that little crease always sneaks out to say hello. But these pictures will wash away into the sands of time, eventually, as such scandals always do. Either that, or Jeb will use his super i-savvy to erase them from all the computers.

Jeb's hair will somehow become an issue, with pundits constantly comparing it to Donald Trump's hair and ruminating on whose hair would win a debate. This won't really be a "gaffe," as they say, because folks will think, "What can a man do about his hair? It's not really Jeb's fault, is it?" But the liberal medias will stick with it. Fortunately those same pundits will have to sit back in amazement as Jeb wins the Hair Wars by perming his hair, creating a spectacular three-foot-diameter afro.

Jeb will absolutely appoint someone stupid to a major cabinet post. Everyone, especially Democrat-leaning writers, will say, "How could Jeb have appointed someone so stupid for such an important post?" But Jeb will not answer those charges. He will stand by his decision, because that is the right thing to do. Then the stupid appointee will do a lot of stupid things, and make stupid decisions. Jeb will continue to stand by his stupid appointee and his stupid decisions, as well as his original stupid decision to appoint the stupid person, because that is the Bush way. But finally external pressure will be too much, and Jeb will dismiss the stupid person on the grounds that the appointee is stupid, and wants to spend more time with their stupid family. But a lot of stupid things will manage to get done before that point, so everyone will win.

Jeb will kill a man while in office. It will be an unprovoked act of wanton violence, such as strangulation or a vicious beating. Even though this killing will be justified, and likely in self-defense, as usual the liberal news outlets will not be able to let it go.

There will emerge a major scandal in which Jeb is accused of misappropriating funds, or Jeb will stretch the meaning of "discretionary budget" to mean far more than it ever has in the past. Columba will spend too much on drapes—something of this ilk. Jeb will find a way to spend a lot of money on something like cologne or carved owls to decorate the White House. The accountability peanut gallery will have a field day.

Finally, most Presidents endure an impeachment threat nowadays, and Jeb will be no exception. Congress will try to impeach Jeb after either the misappropriations scandal or the Columba love triangle or the murder—they'll make a case about anything!—and it won't go far. But a lot of hay will be made, and it will make for good television news chatter. But I do not believe it will go beyond that, at least not before his third term.

Why a President Jeb Needs America, and Vice Versa

———— ⌒ ————

What makes a man worthy of the Office of the Command Seat of the United States?

There are many answers to these questions. He may be a forefather, like the great George Washington, who hewned the office out of a cherry tree and then self-determined if he was to be worthy of that tree. He may be honest, like the noble Abraham Lincoln, who was born, appropriately, in a Lincoln Log cabin at the time of the Gettysburg Address Wars of our nation. There was Franklin Delano Roosevelt, who was known for his great disabledness, and therefore nicknamed "Polio Pete." And there was me, George W. Bush, the quicentenially ideal President in every way that can be measured by the presidential measurers.

Looking at all of these legendary Presidents, what do we have in common? We were all bold men of vision who stood tall, with the exception of Franklin Delano Roosevelt. We were also all War Presidents, the great trials of our countrymen having forged our resolve. All great Presidents were War Presidents. Grover Cleveland will be remembered forever for the Apache wars that smoked the Terrorist

Geronimo out of his teepee into the safety of a reservation, thus protecting a nation. Woodrow Wilson was awarded the great Bronze Prize for his victory in World War I. Both Bush Presidents have been War Presidents, facing the same evil opponent, the nation of Iraq or Afghanistan.

I believe it is highly likely that Jeb will follow in our giant strides of wardom, provided he can find a suitable country or group to start a war with. I have every confidence he will find one, using his own horse sense as well as having the wisdom to surround himself with only the wisest enemy-finders.

But, surprisingly, some say it takes more than dreams and plans of war—no matter how great—to make a man worthy to be a President. It also takes the American people adoring that President, and voting for him. This is where you come in, reading person, if you are American and can vote. If you're Cuban or Canadian or Kamchatkan, you can skip this next section because, by your very un-American nature, you cannot support the next President. In fact, if you are not an American, I'd prefer you stop reading this book right now, and throw it in the water.

Jeb is on the cusp of the nomination. At the time of this writing, he is riding his bicycle around the country, pleading with the Republican Caucusing Lamas atop mountains, and filling out the proper forms to ensure adequate support in the primary nominations across our states. You may have noticed Jeb looks a bit slimmer of late. All of that bicycling around the countryside—as well as walking from village to village through deserts and mountains, his great walking stick keeping his gait steady—has really helped him shed some pounds around his midsection and face. All that's left for him to do now is sing with the gnomes and bullhorn his candidacy from the official campaign announcement Quonset hut. But heck, by the time you're reading this, he's probably already the nominee.

Jeb has been preparing for this moment in history his entire life. Or more accurately, I have been preparing him. I have taught him, mentored him, tortured him, and advised him. I have held him when he broke down sobbing, lifted him up when he couldn't go on being tortured, and I have painted him, both on reverent canvas and on his face when he was asleep many nights during his college years. And I pledge to do all of that again should he be fortunate enough to be elected to be 45.

To put it simply, I have created the Super Candidate who will be the Ultimate President. There will no longer be a need for any other Presidents once he is elected. He will be like the great statue of Honest Abe Lincoln on the hallowed Washington Mall, standing proud for hundreds of years. But instead of ineffective and unmoving stone, he will be a fleshy thing that moves around and makes decisions. And they will be great decisions, ones that will stand for all time as some of the greatest decodings in our nation's history.

He will also, if elected, take time off for vacations.

Jeb is experienced. He has governed the retired state of Florida. Is it comparable to governing the great state of Texas? Probably not, but let's not pick hairs. Governing is a tricky business whatever the state one chooses to rule, and Florida is no exception. Figuring out how to keep the oranges at the proper temperature for both growth and storage is a delicate balance. Keeping the Seminole Linebackers content to sit on their reservations and not rise up to take Florida's capital city has trained him well in the art of both diplomacy and war-making. Keeping Florida out of the great rap wars of the 1980s was another great achievement of Jeb's reign, which I forgot to mention in the "Florida" chapter, but I already wrote that chapter, therefore I will not go back and make any changes or corrections no matter how egregious the omission.

Jeb has a plan. He knows what he must do as President. For one, he knows he must have wise advisors, such as myself. He must build great walls around our country. He must continue to defeat Terror. And as his greatest act, he must dismantle the waste and abuse that is the United States government.

So, Jeb has the training, the experience, and the plan. Does he then deserve the title of 45?

Throughout this book I have attempted to provide the most thoughtful, learned, and exhaustive research ever undertaken in the history of presidential-runner history. I sought to do this for one reason: to determine if Jeb is indeed worthy of the office chair. Did this work help us arrive at the proper conclusion? I believe it did. And what, then, is the unevitable conclusion? Should Jeb be our next President?

The answer is yes.

If you're reading of these pages brought you to a different and wrong conclusion, please read the book again.

Now that we have established the fact that Jeb is destined to be our next leader in the War Room, we must help and support him in his great calling. Jeb cannot complete his journey to the White House alone.

First of all he has to have financial support. I ask all you corporations reading this, search into your hearts and give to Jeb's super PAC fund. I realize you are not humans with an actual heart, but you are just as important—if not more important—because your hearts can be filled with so much more money than a human heart. Don't worry about campaign donation limits. This is a human worry, and remember that you are like a superhuman impervious to these limits.

Wonderful new rules concerning these new PAC things get around any limit. Koch brothers, there's nothing to hold you back anymore. Oil companies, if you want Jeb's blessing to drill where you please, technically we can't promise you anything, but seeing your name at the top of the Right to Rise PAC donation list would not be a bad place to start the conversation. NRA, maybe you would like to see the Second Amendment rise to first place? You know what to do. Click here to donate.

Having said all of that, and sharing the good news of our nation's improved campaign laws, the fact is that even a billion dollars won't do it all by itself. Money alone is not the answer.

Jeb needs your support, GOP Caucus Members. Phase two of support starts with you, supporting him to be the grand marshal of the great GOP parade, which will end with Jeb triumphantly battling it out with the Democratic grand marshal in the general election. If you support him to that point, your job will be done. And you can just sit back and enjoy the fight.

I don't believe there are any rules that prohibit Jeb from being the Democratic nominee as well. So, if you're on the other side of the political fence, which is very difficult for me to understand, imagine, or respect, then why don't you save us a lot of trouble and also nominate Jeb on the Democrat Caucusers' forms? This will make the general election much easier for Jeb.

After that, it's in your hands, Electoral Voters. You have the power to send Jeb to his final seating-place in the Oval Office. Listen to all the voters out there in the popular election. Especially to those who have read and memorized this book and followed their hearts, moved by the touching facts outlined herein.

The rest of us? We can all vote, and rest assured our vote will count, perhaps even more than others'. But the final decision rests with the Electorate College and their best judgment. And perhaps the Supreme Court as well. But with luck and providence, their judgment and our judgment will align up nicely and coincide with destiny. If this great and momentous achievement is achieved, we will all stand proud on Election Day and honor a knucklehead in the White House—a knucklehead that I will be proud to call my brother.

Acknowledgments

————— ⌀ —————

No man can write a book alone. I have come close with *45*, and hesitate to acknowledge anyone else. But I must admit there are some, however insignificant, who made very small contributions to this fine work. Scott Dikkers and Peter Hilleren certainly deserve to be mentioned, as they are very affordable ghost writers. Sean Desmond, Libby Burton, and Liz Connor at the Hachette Book Group contributed invaluable book-making and book-writing expertise. Daniel Greenberg and Tim Wojcik helped me communicate with and understand the strange book-creating people I mentioned before. Eric Stassen and Matthew Visconage provided exemplary standing ability, in evidence on the book's front and back covers. And no budding artist such as myself could have created such beautiful works of art for this book without the superb ghost-painting of Irvan Satria. Finally, for this book's audio edition, Kristen Hagopian never wavered in her announcering, and Michele McGonigle set bold deadlines through the sending out of "type-e" mail. Semper Fi.

About the Authors

———— ❧ ————

SCOTT DIKKERS is a #1 *New York Times* bestselling author who founded the world's first humor website, theonion.com, and served as its editor in chief for many years. His work has won the Thurber Prize for American Humor, a Peabody, and over thirty Webby Awards.

A former writer for *The Onion*, PETER HILLEREN is a public radio producer whose top-ten iTunes George W. Bush parody podcast "Weekly Radio Address" led to his partnering with Dikkers to create *Destined for Destiny*.